Just Joking

ARCTURUS

This edition published in 2018 by Arcturus Publishing Limited
26/27 Bickels Yard, 151–153 Bermondsey Street,
London SE1 3HA

Copyright © Arcturus Holdings Limited

All rights reserved. No part of this publication may be reproduced,
stored in a retrieval system, or transmitted, in any form or by any means,
electronic, mechanical, photocopying, recording or otherwise, without
prior written permission in accordance with the provisions of the
Copyright Act 1956 (as amended). Any person or persons who do any
unauthorised act in relation to this publication may be liable to criminal
prosecution and civil claims for damages.

ISBN: 978-1-78428-614-9
CH005153NT
Supplier 29, Date 0418, Print run 7188

Written by Lisa Regan
Illustrated by Shutterstock
Designed by Trudi Webb
Edited by Tracey Kelly

Printed in China

CONTENTS

TERRIBLE TRAVEL

HOW DO LIGHTHOUSE KEEPERS COMMUNICATE WITH EACH OTHER?

WITH SHINE LANGUAGE!

WHAT CAN FLY UNDERWATER?

A WASP IN A SUBMARINE!

WHAT DO YOU USE TO CUT THE OCEAN IN TWO?

A SEASAW!

WHAT IS BIG, FURRY, AND FLIES?

A HOT-AIR BABOON!

WHAT DO THEY SING ON YOUR BIRTHDAY IN ICELAND?

"FREEZE A JOLLY GOOD FELLOW!"

WHEN IS A BOAT LIKE A PILE OF SNOW?

WHEN IT'S ADRIFT!

WHAT FALLS AT THE NORTH POLE BUT NEVER GETS HURT?

SNOW!

WHAT DO YOU CALL A STRANDED POLAR BEAR?

ICE-OLATED!

WHAT DO YOU CALL A HAPPY ONE-LEGGED PIRATE?

A HOP-TIMIST!

WHY WAS THE PIRATE FEELING SAD?

LONG TIME, NO SEA.

WHAT MUSIC DO PIRATES LISTEN TO?

SOLE MUSIC!

HOW MUCH DO PIRATES PAY TO GET THEIR EARS PIERCED?

A BUCK AN EAR!

WHAT HAPPENS WHEN YOU THROW A WHITE ROCK INTO THE RED SEA?

IT GETS WET!

WHY DO SEAGULLS LIVE BY THE SEA?

BECAUSE IF THEY LIVED BY THE BAY, THEY'D BE BAGELS!

WHAT IS FLUFFY AND GREEN?

A SEASICK SHEEP!

WHAT DO CLOWNS WEAR TO GO SWIMMING?

GIGGLES!

19

WHEN'S THE BEST TIME TO BUY A PIRATE SHIP?

WHEN THEY'RE ON SAIL!

HOW DOES A PIRATE TRAVEL WHEN HE'S ON LAND?

BY CARRRRRRR!

WHY CAN'T YOU TAKE A PHOTO OF A PIRATE WITH A WOODEN LEG?

BECAUSE WOODEN LEGS DON'T TAKE PHOTOS!

WHAT DID THE PIRATE SAY WHEN HE TRAPPED HIS WOODEN LEG IN THE FREEZER?

"SHIVER ME TIMBERS!"

WHAT'S THE BEST WAY TO CROSS THE OCEAN?

BY TAXI-CRAB!

WHAT KEEPS ON RUNNING WITHOUT GETTING TIRED?

A RIVER!

WHAT DO YOU GET IF YOU MEET A SHARK IN THE ARCTIC OCEAN?

FROSTBITE!

WHY WOULD YOU TAKE A BASEBALL GLOVE ON A SURFING TRIP?

SO YOU CAN CATCH A WAVE!

TEACHER: HAVE YOU CONSIDERED A CAREER AS AN AIRLINE PILOT?

JACOB: DO YOU THINK I'M THAT CLEVER?

TEACHER: WELL, YOU ALWAYS HAVE YOUR HEAD IN THE CLOUDS!

WHAT IS THE FASTEST COUNTRY IN THE WORLD?

RUSHA!

WHAT DID ONE MOUNTAIN SAY TO THE OTHER?

"YOU'RE LOOKING A LITTLE PEAKY!"

WHERE DO EGGS GO FOR A WEEKEND BREAK?

NEW YOLK!

WHY SHOULD YOU NEVER ARGUE ON A HOT-AIR BALLOON RIDE?

YOU DON'T WANT TO FALL OUT!

WHICH ANIMAL WAS THE FIRST IN SPACE?

THE COW WHO JUMPED OVER THE MOON!

WHERE IS HADRIAN'S WALL?

AROUND HADRIAN'S GARDEN!

WHAT KIND OF HOUSE WEIGHS THE LEAST?

A LIGHTHOUSE!

27

WHAT DO YOU CALL A TOY TRAIN SET?

A PLAY STATION!

WHY DON'T ELEPHANTS TRAVEL BY TRAIN?

THEY DON'T LIKE PUTTING THEIR TRUNKS ON THE LUGGAGE RACK!

WHY DID THE TRAIN DRIVER GET FIRED?

HE WAS TOO EASILY SIDE-TRACKED!

WHERE CAN YOU BUY A TRAIN TERMINUS?

AN END-OF-LINE SALE!

WHEN IS A SAILOR LIKE A PLANK OF WOOD?

WHEN HE'S ABOARD!

WHAT DID THE SAILOR THINK AS HE FELL OVERBOARD?

WATER WAY TO GO!

WHAT KIND OF HAIRSTYLE DO SAILORS HAVE?

A CREW CUT!

WHY WON'T YOU STARVE IF YOU GET SHIPWRECKED BY A BEACH?

YOU CAN EAT ALL THE SAND WHICH IS THERE!

WHY DID THE BRIDGE GET ANGRY?

BECAUSE PEOPLE WERE ALWAYS CROSSING IT!

WHEN IS A CAR NOT A CAR?

WHEN IT TURNS INTO A DRIVEWAY.

WHAT DO YOU GET IF YOU RUN BEHIND A CAR?

EXHAUSTED!

WHY DID THE LITTLE CAR STOP WHEN IT SAW THE MONSTER TRUCK?

IT HAD A NERVOUS BREAKDOWN!

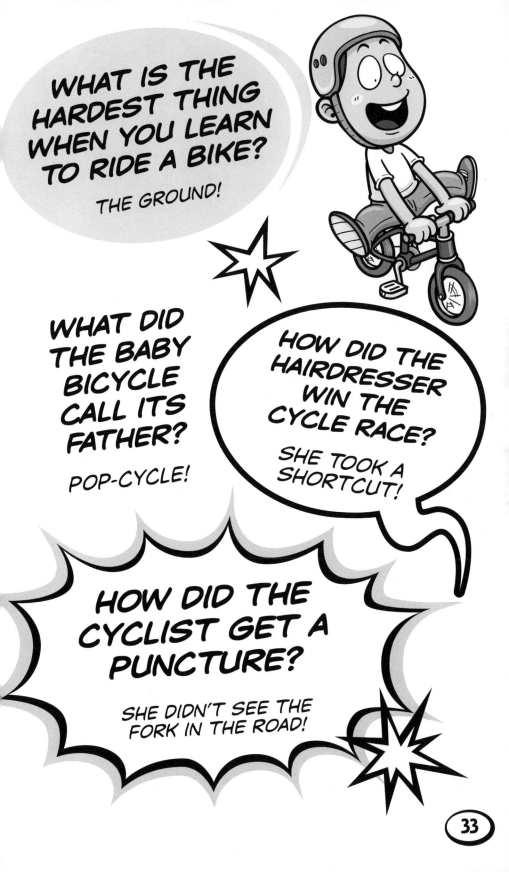

WHAT DO YOU CALL A LAZY BABY KANGAROO?

A POUCH POTATO!

WHAT DO YOU CALL A BOOMERANG THAT DOESN'T COME BACK?

A STICK!

WHY DO KANGAROOS HATE BAD WEATHER?

BECAUSE THE KIDS HAVE TO PLAY INDOORS!

WHAT ANIMAL CAN JUMP HIGHER THAN SYDNEY OPERA HOUSE?

ALL ANIMALS, BECAUSE THE OPERA HOUSE CAN'T JUMP!

WHY DO THE FRENCH LOVE TO EAT SNAILS?

THEY DON'T LIKE FAST FOOD!

WHAT'S PURPLE AND FISHY AND FOUND OFF THE COAST OF AUSTRALIA?

THE GRAPE BARRIER REEF!

WHICH CAPITAL CITY IS GROWING AT THE FASTEST RATE?

DUBLIN!

DID YOU HEAR ABOUT THE MAN WHO JUMPED OFF A BRIDGE IN PARIS?

HE WAS IN SEINE!

39

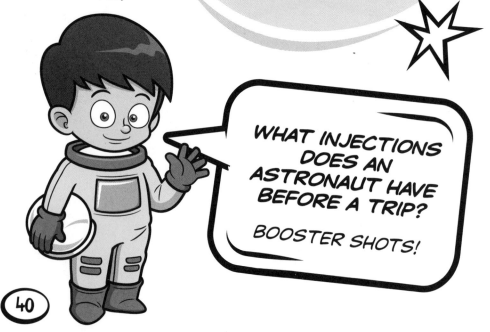

43

HOW DO TRAINS HEAR?

WITH THEIR ENGINE-EARS!

WHY DID THE SPY GET ARRESTED AT THE STATION?

HE WAS TRYING TO COVER HIS TRACKS!

IF THERE ARE TEN CATS ON A TRAIN AND ONE GETS OFF, HOW MANY ARE LEFT?

NONE, THEY'RE ALL COPYCATS!

DID YOU HEAR ABOUT THE COMMUTER WHO ATE GUM EVERY MORNING?

HE CAUGHT THE CHEW-CHEW TRAIN!

WHAT DO YOU CALL AN OGRE WITH A TWISTED ANKLE?

A HOBLIN GOBLIN!

WHY DIDN'T THE PIXIE INVITE HIS SCHOOL FRIEND FOR SUPPER?

HIS MOTHER COULDN'T STAND THE GOBLIN!

WHERE DOES A GOBLIN GO SHOPPING?

AT THE GROSSERY STORE!

HOW DOES AN OGRE CLEAN THE BATHROOM?

HE USES DISIN-SHREK-TANT!

WHAT DO YOU GET IF YOU PUT A WIZARD AT THE NORTH POLE?

A COLD SPELL!

WHAT DID THE GOLDEN SNITCH SAY WHEN HARRY POTTER WAS BITTEN BY A MOSQUITO?

QUIDDITCHING!

WHAT DO YOU CALL A WIZARD FROM OUTER SPACE?

A FLYING SORCERER!

WHY DID THE WIZARD FLUNK SCHOOL?

HE WAS TERRIBLE AT SPELLING!

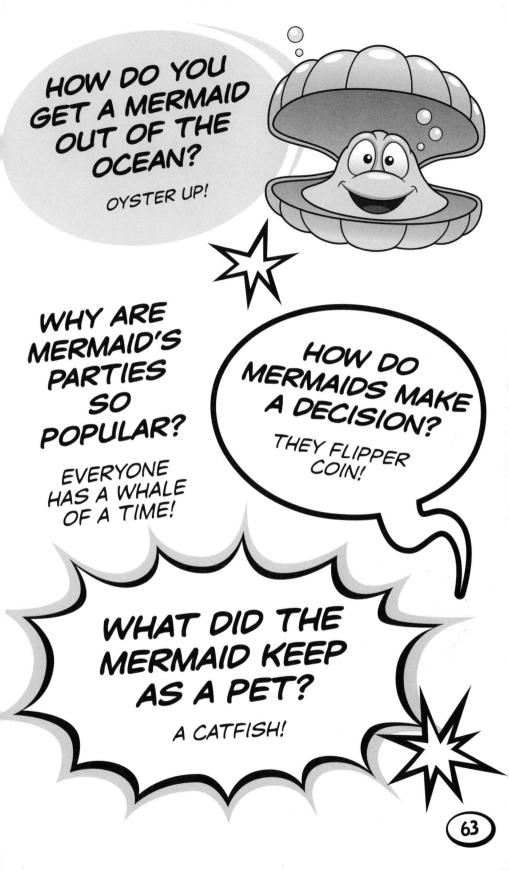

63

69

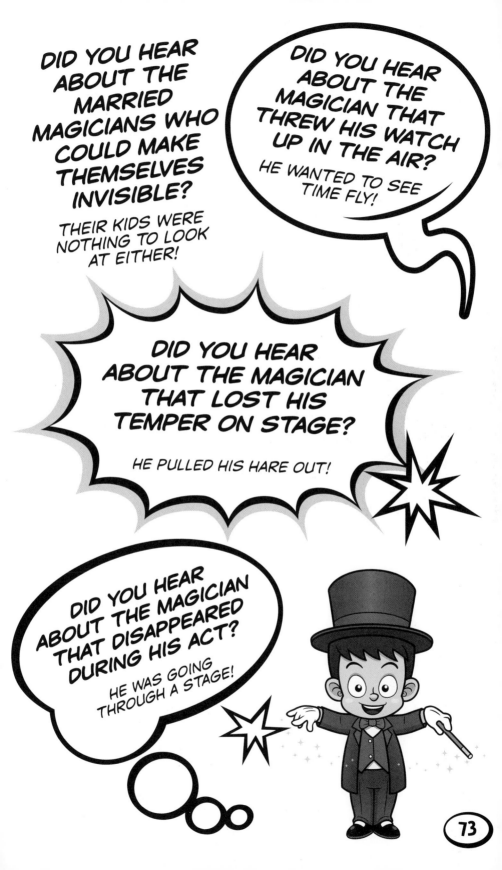

WHAT HAS SHARP TEETH AND LIVES AT THE END OF THE RAINBOW?

THE CROC OF GOLD!

WHY DID LITTLE MISS MUFFET NEED A MAP?

BECAUSE SHE'D LOST HER WHEY!

WHY DID RAPUNZEL GO WILD AT PARTIES?

SHE LIKED TO LET HER HAIR DOWN!

WHO TOLD THE BIG, BAD WOLF HE WAS UGLY AND SMELLY?

LITTLE RUDE RIDING HOOD!

HOW LONG SHOULD AN ELF'S LEGS BE?

JUST LONG ENOUGH TO REACH THE GROUND!

HOW MANY ELVES DOES IT TAKE TO CHANGE A LIGHT BULB?

TEN: ONE TO TWIST THE BULB AND NINE TO STAND ON EACH OTHER'S SHOULDERS!

WHAT DO ELVES USE TO SERVE ICE CREAM?

A MICROSCOOP!

WHAT DO ELVES USE TO MAKE THEIR SANDWICHES?

SHORTBREAD!

77

DO YOU KNOW THE FAIRY TALE ABOUT THE FROG PRINCE?

REDDIT...

WHY DID GOLDILOCKS STIR THE PORRIDGE REALLY HARD?

BECAUSE DADDY BEAR TOLD HER TO BEAT IT!

WHAT DID HANSEL AND GRETEL SAY WHEN THEY BROKE THE WITCH'S HOUSE?

"THAT'S THE WAY THE COOKIE CRUMBLES!"

WHAT'S WOODEN, HAS A LONG NOSE, AND GOES BOING?

PINOCCHIO ON A BUNGEE JUMP!

WHAT DID THE WITCH DO WHEN HER BROOMSTICK BROKE?

SHE WITCH-HIKED!

WHO IS IN CHARGE OF THE LIGHTING AT HALLOWEEN?

THE LIGHTS WITCH!

WHY DON'T BAD-TEMPERED WITCHES RIDE BROOMSTICKS?

THEY'RE AFRAID OF FLYING OFF THE HANDLE!

WHAT DOES A WITCH BUY AT THE HAIRDRESSER'S?

SCARE SPRAY!

85

WHY DID LUCIUS MALFOY CROSS THE ROAD TWICE?

BECAUSE HE WAS A DOUBLE-CROSSER!

HOW DO DEATH EATERS FRESHEN THEIR BREATH?

WITH DEMENTOS!

WHAT KIND OF BREAKFAST CEREAL DO THEY SERVE AT HOGWARTS?

HUFFLEPUFFS!

WHAT DO YOU CALL QUIDDITCH PLAYERS WHO SHARE A DORM?

BROOM-MATES!

WHAT'S THE DIFFERENCE BETWEEN A STORM AND A HORSE?

ONE RAINS DOWN, THE OTHER IS REINED UP!

WHAT DID THE TORNADO SAY TO THE SPORTS CAR?

"WANT TO GO FOR A SPIN?"

WHAT KIND OF CLOTHES DO BLACK CLOUDS WEAR?

THUNDERWEAR!

WHAT'S THE DIFFERENCE BETWEEN A STORM CLOUD AND A BEAR RAIDING A BEEHIVE?

ONE POURS WITH RAIN AND THE OTHER ROARS WITH PAIN!

WHY CAN'T PINE TREES SEW?

THEY ALWAYS DROP THEIR NEEDLES!

DID YOU KNOW THAT I CAN CUT DOWN A TREE JUST BY STARING AT IT?

IT'S TRUE – I SAW IT WITH MY OWN EYES!

WHERE DO SAPLINGS GO TO LEARN?

ELEMEN-TREE SCHOOL!

WHAT'S GREEN AND HAS LEAVES AND A TRUNK?

A HOUSEPLANT GOING AWAY ON A LONG TRIP!

95

WHAT IS ON TOP OF A SNOWMAN'S BED?

A BLANKET OF SNOW!

WHAT DID THE POLAR BEAR SAY TO THE MELTING ICE?

"YOU NEED TO COOL DOWN!"

WHERE DO SNOWMEN UPLOAD THEIR WEBSITES?

ON THE WINTERNET!

WHAT HAPPENED TO THE SNOWMAN IN THE SPRING?

HE MADE A POOL OF HIMSELF!

99

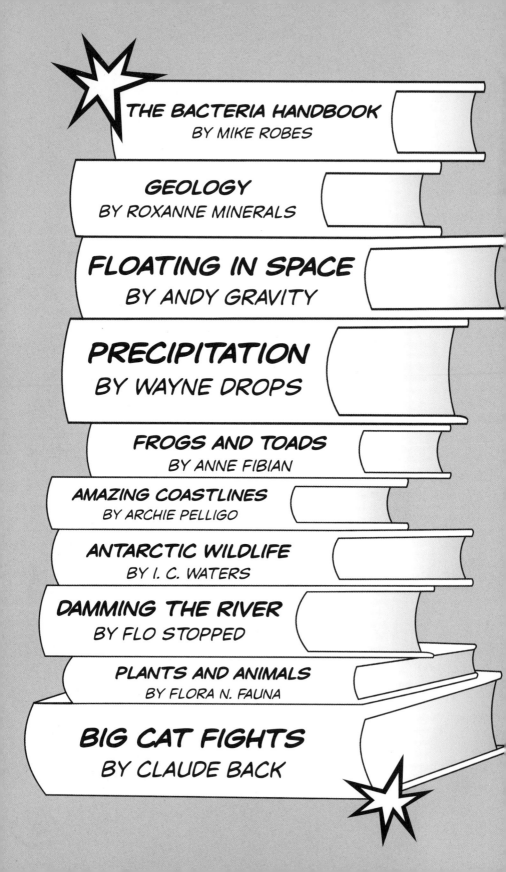

WHERE DO WEATHERMEN GO FOR A DRINK?

THE CLOSEST ISOBAR!

WHAT DID ONE HURRICANE SAY TO THE OTHER?

"I HAVE MY EYE ON YOU!"

WHAT DO YOU SAY WHEN IT RAINS DUCKS AND CHICKENS?

"FOWL WEATHER, ISN'T IT?"

WHAT DID ONE TORNADO SAY TO THE OTHER?

"LET'S TWIST AGAIN LIKE WE DID LAST SUMMER!"

WHAT DID THE DIVER SHOUT WHEN HE SWAM INTO A SEAWEED FOREST?

"KELP!"

DO FISH LIKE TO WATCH BASEBALL?

YES—THERE ARE 20,000 LEAGUES UNDER THE SEA!

WHAT ARE LITTLE SEA CREATURES MOST AFRAID OF?

SQUID-NAPPERS!

WHY DO FISH IN A SCHOOL ALL SWIM IN THE SAME DIRECTION?

THEY'RE PLAYING SALMON SAYS!

WHY ARE FROGS ALWAYS HAPPY?
BECAUSE THEY CAN EAT WHATEVER BUGS THEM!

WHAT DID THE COW SAY WHEN IT WAS HUNGRY?
"THISTLE HAVE TO DO!"

WHAT DID THE SPIDER SAY WHEN ITS WEB GOT BROKEN?
"DARN IT!"

WHY DO MALE DEER NEED BRACES?
BECAUSE THEY HAVE BUCK TEETH!

CINDY: DID YOU KNOW IT'S RAINING CATS AND DOGS OUT THERE?

MINDY: I KNOW, I JUST STEPPED IN A POODLE!

WHAT'S THE DIFFERENCE BETWEEN WEATHER AND CLIMATE?

YOU CAN'T WEATHER A TREE, BUT YOU CAN CLIMATE!

WHY SHOULDN'T YOU ARGUE WITH A WEATHERMAN?

HE MIGHT STORM OUT ON YOU!

WHY DID THE MAN TAKE HIS WALLET OUT INTO THE STORM?

HE WAS HOPING FOR SOME CHANGE IN THE WEATHER!

WHAT GOES SNAP, CRACKLE, POP?

A FIREFLY WITH A SHORT CIRCUIT!

WHAT'S THE LARGEST MOTH IN THE WORLD?

A MAMMOTH!

WHAT DID THE WORM SAY TO HER SON WHEN HE CAME HOME LATE?

"WHERE IN EARTH HAVE YOU BEEN?"

WHAT DO YOU CALL A FLY WITH NO WINGS?

A WALK!

WHERE DO BEES GO WHEN THEY NEED TO USE THE BATHROOM?

THE BP STATION!

WHAT DO YOU CALL AN INTERFERING BEE?

A BUZZYBODY!

HOW CAN YOU TELL A WORM'S HEAD FROM ITS TAIL?

TICKLE THE MIDDLE, AND SEE WHICH END LAUGHS!

WHAT DID THE BEE SHOUT WHEN THE HIVE WAS UNDER ATTACK?

"BEE-WARE!"

FUNNY FAMILY

WHY WAS THE YOUNGEST OF SEVEN CHILDREN LATE FOR SCHOOL?

BECAUSE THE ALARM WAS SET FOR SIX!

TEACHER: WHAT IS THE PLURAL OF BABY?

FRANCES: TWINS!

TEACHER: DID YOUR MOTHER HELP YOU WITH YOUR HOMEWORK?

CHARLIE: NO, I GOT IT WRONG ALL BY MYSELF!

DAD: WHY DIDN'T YOU COME STRAIGHT HOME FROM SCHOOL?

SEBASTIAN: BECAUSE WE LIVE AROUND THE CORNER!

WHY DID DAD TAKE HIS RAZOR TO SPORTS DAY?

HE WANTED TO SHAVE A FEW SECONDS OFF HIS TIME!

EMILY: DAD, I GOT AN A IN SPELLING!

DAD: YOU FOOL, THERE ISN'T AN A IN SPELLING!

GRANDMA: I HEAR YOU'VE BEEN MISSING SCHOOL?

BRADLEY: THAT'S A LIE. I HAVEN'T MISSED IT ONE BIT!

DID YOU HEAR ABOUT THE EMBARRASSING TWINS IN THE LONG DISTANCE RACE?

ONE RAN IN SHORT BURSTS, THE OTHER RAN IN BURST SHORTS!

133

MY BROTHER IS SO DUMB, HE FOUND THREE MILK CARTONS IN A FIELD AND THOUGHT IT WAS A COW'S NEST!

MY BROTHER IS SO DUMB, HE DRINKS HOT CHOCOLATE AT NIGHT SO HE WILL HAVE SWEET DREAMS!

MY BROTHER IS SO DUMB, HE THINKS GLUTEUS MAXIMUS IS A ROMAN EMPEROR!

MY BROTHER IS SO DUMB, HE WENT LOOKING FOR A HILLY LAKE SO HE COULD WATER SKI!

NICK: MY DAD HAD TO GO TO COURT FOR STEALING A CALENDAR.

RICK: WHAT HAPPENED?

NICK: HE GOT TWELVE MONTHS!

WHY DID DAD RUN AROUND HIS BED?

HE WANTED TO CATCH UP ON HIS SLEEP!

CHRISTINE: MY DAD CAN JUGGLE EGGSHELLS, YESTERDAY'S NEWSPAPER, AND AN EMPTY BOX!

EUGENE: THAT'S GARBAGE!

RAQUEL: WHY DOES YOUR DAD WEAR TWO SWEATERS FOR GOLF?

MICHELLE: IN CASE HE GETS A HOLE IN ONE!

WINNIE: WHY IS THERE A PLANE OUTSIDE YOUR BEDROOM DOOR?

VINNIE: I MUST HAVE LEFT THE LANDING LIGHT ON!

WHAT KIND OF MONSTER LIVES IN YOUR BROTHER'S ROOM?

THE LOCH MESS MONSTER!

JAN: HOW CAN YOU FIT TWENTY FRIENDS IN YOUR ROOM AT ONCE AND STILL PLAY A GAME?

STAN: WE'RE PLAYING SQUASH!

DAD: THERE'S A BURGLAR DOWNSTAIRS EATING THE CAKE YOUR SISTER BAKED.

HUGH: SHOULD I CALL THE POLICE OR AN AMBULANCE?

LITTLE SISTER: WHY IS OUR GOLDFISH ORANGE?

BIG BROTHER: BECAUSE THE WATER MAKES IT RUSTY!

DID YOU HEAR ABOUT THE GUPPY THAT WENT TO HOLLYWOOD?

IT BECAME A STARFISH!

KIM: WHY IS YOUR DRAWING OF A FISH SO TINY?

TIM: I'VE DRAWN IT TO SCALE!

WHAT IS STRANGER THAN SEEING A CAT FISH?

SEEING A GOLDFISH BOWL!

141

DAD: YOU'VE BEEN WALKING SIDEWAYS EVER SINCE YOU CAME HOME FROM THE HOSPITAL.

HANNAH: THEY SAID MY MEDICINE MIGHT HAVE SIDE EFFECTS...

BOBBY: WHAT'S THE DIFFERENCE BETWEEN A HILL AND A PILL?

ROBBIE: A HILL IS HARD TO GET UP, BUT A PILL IS HARD TO GET DOWN.

WHAT DID THE MOTHER BROOM SAY TO HER SON?

IT'S TIME TO GO TO SWEEP!

WHAT CAN YOU GIVE AND KEEP AT THE SAME TIME?

A COLD!

142

WHAT DO CATS EAT ON HOT DAYS?

MICE-CREAM CONES!

WHY ARE CATS SO GOOD AT EXAMS?

THEY GIVE PURRFECT ANSWERS!

HOW DO CATS KNOW WHAT IS GOING ON IN THE WORLD?

THEY READ THE MEWSPAPER!

WHY ARE THERE MORE GHOST CATS THAN GHOST DOGS?

BECAUSE EVERY CAT HAS NINE LIVES!

145

147

149

WHEN SHOULD A MOUSE STAY INDOORS?

WHEN IT'S RAINING CATS AND DOGS!

WHO ARE SMALL, FURRY, AND FANTASTIC AT SWORD FIGHTING?

THE THREE MOUSEKETEERS!

WHY SHOULDN'T YOU WORRY IF YOU SEE MICE IN YOUR HOME?

THEY'RE PROBABLY DOING THE MOUSEWORK!

WHAT DO YOU DO IF YOUR PET MOUSE FALLS IN THE SINK?

GIVE IT MOUSE-TO-MOUSE RESUSCITATION!

CASEY: WHY IS YOUR SISTER SO GOOD AT SPORT?

STACEY: SHE HAS ATHLETE'S FOOT!

WHY DID THE JOGGER EAT ON THE RUN?

SHE LOVED FAST FOOD!

AMANDA: IS YOUR BROTHER ANY GOOD AT RUNNING?

MIRANDA: HE'S SO SLOW HE RAN A BATH AND CAME SECOND!

WHEN IS A BASKETBALL PLAYER LIKE A BABY?

WHEN HE DRIBBLES!

157

LITTLE PENCIL: YOU LOOK AS THOUGH YOU'VE PUT ON WEIGHT, DAD.

DADDY PENCIL: YOU'RE VERY BLUNT!

WHY WAS THE LITTLE BROOM LATE FOR SCHOOL?

IT OVERSWEPT!

WHY WAS THE LITTLE ICEBERG JUST LIKE HIS DAD?

BECAUSE HE WAS A CHIP OFF THE COLD BLOCK!

WHAT DID THE MOTHER DOG SAY TO THE PUPPY?

"WE'RE HAVING DINNER SOON, DON'T EAT TOO MUCH HOMEWORK!"

CLARK: WHY IS YOUR GRANDPA DRESSED AS A CLOWN?

MARK: JEST FOR FUN!

HOW DO YOU MAKE ANTIFREEZE?

HIDE HER COAT AND GLOVES!

MICKEY: OUR MOTHER HAS NAMED US ALL AFTER MEMBERS OF OUR FAMILY.

NICKY: IS THAT WHY YOUR BIG BROTHER IS CALLED UNCLE JOE?

DID YOU HEAR THAT UNCLE BOB LOST HIS WIG ON THE ROLLER COASTER?

IT WAS A HAIR-RAISING RIDE!

169

WHAT HAPPENED TO THE ROYAL CHICKEN THAT COULDN'T LAY EGGS?
THE KING HAD HER EGGS-ECUTED!

WHY DID THE KING VISIT THE DENTIST?
TO HAVE HIS TEETH CROWNED!

WHAT DID KING HENRY VIII DO WHENEVER HE BURPED?
HE ISSUED A ROYAL PARDON!

WHY DID EVERYONE IN 19TH-CENTURY ENGLAND CARRY AN UMBRELLA?
BECAUSE QUEEN VICTORIA'S REIGN LASTED FOR 64 YEARS!

179

WHAT DID THE COLONISTS WEAR AT THE BOSTON TEA PARTY?

TEA-SHIRTS!

WHY DIDN'T GEORGE WASHINGTON BOTHER GOING TO BED?

BECAUSE HE COULDN'T LIE!

WHAT KIND OF TEA WERE THE COLONISTS LOOKING FOR?

LIBER-TEA!

WHERE DID THE PILGRIMS LAND WHEN THEY ARRIVED IN AMERICA?

ON THE BEACH!

193

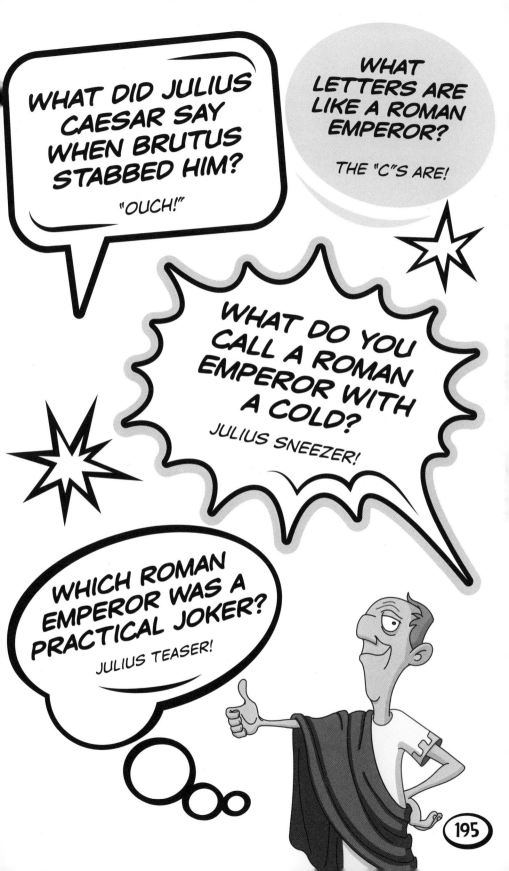

195

197

WHY DID THE ARCHER CHANGE HIS CAREER?

HE FOUND HIS JOB TOO ARROWING!

WHAT WOULD YOU GET HANGING FROM CASTLE WALLS?

TIRED ARMS!

WHY DID THE HANGMAN'S WIFE ASK FOR A DIVORCE?

HER HUSBAND WAS A PAIN IN THE NECK!

WHY DID SOLDIERS FIRE ARROWS FROM THE CASTLE?

THEY WERE TRYING TO GET THEIR POINT ACROSS!

203

WHICH ENGLISHMAN INVENTED FRACTIONS?

HENRY THE EIGHTH!

WHO INVENTED MATCHES?

SOME BRIGHT SPARK!

WHAT HAPPENED WHEN THE WHEEL WAS INVENTED?

IT CAUSED A REVOLUTION!

WHAT HAPPENED WHEN ELECTRICITY WAS FIRST DISCOVERED?

PEOPLE GOT A NASTY SHOCK!

DID YOU HEAR ABOUT THE UNEMBALMED ANCIENT EGYPTIAN DISCOVERY?

IT SPHINX!

WHAT WAS THE SCORE AT THE ANCIENT EGYPTIAN SOCCER GAME?

ONE-NILE!

WHERE DO EGYPTIAN MUMMIES GO FOR A SWIM?

THE DEAD SEA!

IN WHICH PART OF A TOMB DID THE ANCIENT EGYPTIANS BURY THE DEAD?

IN THE PYRA-MIDDLE!

WHICH ANCIENT GREEK WAS THE BEST OF THE BUNCH?

ALEXANDER THE GRAPE!

WHY WAS THE BULLHEADED CREATURE NOT ALLOWED TO VOTE?

BECAUSE IT WAS ONLY A MINOR-TAUR!

WHICH FRUIT LAUNCHED A THOUSAND SHIPS?

MELON OF TROY!

WHAT MOVIE DID THE ANCIENT GREEKS LIKE BEST?

TROY STORY!

SILLY CELEBRATIONS

WHY CAN'T YOU TAKE A TURKEY TO CHURCH?

BECAUSE THEY USE SUCH FOWL LANGUAGE!

WHEN DOES CHRISTMAS COME BEFORE THANKSGIVING?

IN THE DICTIONARY!

WHAT SMELLS THE BEST AT A THANKSGIVING DINNER?

YOUR NOSE!

WHAT SHOULD YOU WEAR TO THANKSGIVING DINNER?

A HAR-VEST!

WHY IS DRACULA SO UNPOPULAR?

BECAUSE HE'S A PAIN IN THE NECK!

WHAT'S THE SWEETEST, SQUISHIEST, SCARIEST DAY OF THE YEAR?

MARSHMALLOWEEN!

WHAT DO BIRDS DO ON HALLOWEEN?

THEY GO TRICK-OR-TWEETING!

WHAT FOOD DO GHOSTS LOVE THE MOST?

ICE SCREAM!

225

WHO DRESSES IN RED AND WHITE, AND IS A DANGER IN THE WATER?

SANTA JAWS!

HOW MUCH DID SANTA PAY FOR HIS SLEIGH?

NOTHING, IT WAS ON THE HOUSE!

WHAT DO SNOWMEN SING TO SANTA CLAUS?

"FREEZE A JOLLY GOOD FELLOW!"

WHAT DO YOU SHOUT WHEN SANTA TAKES THE ROLL CALL?

"PRESENT!"

229

WHAT DID THE WOODCUTTER'S WIFE SAY TO HER HUSBAND ON DECEMBER 1ST?

"NOT MANY CHOPPING DAYS LEFT UNTIL CHRISTMAS!"

HOW DID JACK FROST BREAK HIS WRIST?

HE FELL OFF HIS ICICLE!

HAVE YOU HEARD THE SILLY STORY ABOUT A GIANT MINCE PIE?

IT'S VERY HARD TO SWALLOW.

WHO DELIVERS PRESENTS TO PETS?

SANTA CLAWS!

WHY DID THE GHOST GO UP THE STAIRS?

TO RAISE ITS SPIRITS!

WHAT DOES A SHORT-SIGHTED GHOST NEED?

SPOOK-TACLES!

WHAT CAN YOU HEAR AT HALLOWEEN SAYING, "BITE, SLURP, OUCH!"?

A VAMPIRE WITH A TOOTHACHE!

WHY COULDN'T THE GHOST FIND ITS DAD?

BECAUSE HE WAS TRANSPARENT!

WHAT DID THE SKELETON WRITE IN HER VALENTINE CARD?

"I LOVE EVERY BONE IN YOUR BODY!"

WHAT DID THE MAGNET SAY TO HER BOYFRIEND?

"YOU'RE VERY ATTRACTIVE!"

WHAT DID THE STAG SAY TO HIS GIRLFRIEND?

"I LOVE YOU DEERLY!"

WHAT DID THE GYMNAST SAY TO HER VALENTINE?

"I'M HEAD OVER HEELS IN LOVE WITH YOU!"

WHO DID FRANKENSTEIN TAKE TO THE HALLOWEEN DANCE?

HIS GHOULFRIEND!

WHY DID THE VAMPIRE'S MEAL GIVE HIM HEARTBURN?

BECAUSE IT WAS A STAKE SANDWICH!

DID YOU HEAR ABOUT THE STUPID VAMPIRE?

HE WAS A REAL SUCKER!

WHAT FOOD DO SKELETONS LIKE THE BEST?

SPARERIBS!

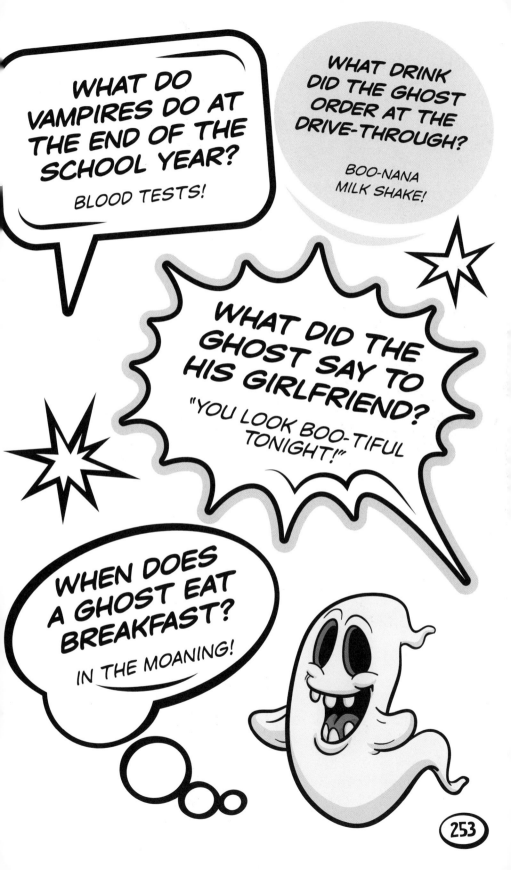

WHY IS IT SO COLD AT CHRISTMAS?

BECAUSE IT'S DECEMBRRRR!

WHAT DO YOU CALL SOMEONE WHO STEALS GIFT WRAP FROM THE RICH AND GIVES IT TO THE POOR?

RIBBON HOOD!

WHAT DID MRS. CLAUS SAY WHEN SANTA SHED A TEAR?

"DON'T GET SO SANTA-MENTAL, DARLING!"

WHAT KIND OF BALL DOESN'T BOUNCE?

A SNOWBALL!